I0485260

SALES

MANAGEMENT

:: Author ::

KINCHIT PARESHBHAI SHAH

(M.COM., C.A. – CPT., P.G.D.T.P(Gold Medalist)., SLET)

PUBLISHED BY

Chakravarti Sidhdhharaj Jaysinh International
Publishing House
HQ. At & Po. Chaveli., Ta- Chansma,
Dist- Patan, North Gujarat, India, Asia.
www.iphouseindia.com

SALES MANAGEMENT

First Publication: 20TH FEBRUARY, 2015

Copyright: Author
(c) KINCHIT PARESHBHAI SHAH

ISBN:- 978-15-08712-53-4

Price: Rs.750/- INDIA
       $ 15 OUTSIDE INDIA

PUBLISHED BY

Chakravarti Sidhdhharaj Jaysinh International Publishing House
HQ. At & Po. Chaveli., Ta- Chansma,
Dist- Patan, North Gujarat, India, Asia.
www.iphouseindia.com

Dedicated
to
my
Parents

Sales Management - An Overview

The art of meeting and exceeding the sales goals of an organization through effective planning, controlling, budgeting and leadership refers to sales management.

Sales Management helps the organization to achieve the sales targets efficiently.

Process of Sales Management

1. Sales Planning

- Marketers must plan things well in advance for the best results. It is essential to have concrete plans. Mere guess works do not help in business.

- Know your product well. Sales professionals must know the USPs and benefits of the product for the consumers to believe them.

- Identify your target market.

- Sales Planning makes the products available to the end users at the right time and at the right place.

- Sales Planning helps the marketers to analyze the customer demands and respond efficiently to fluctuations in the market.

- Devise appropriate strategies to increase the sales of the products.

2. Sales Reporting

- Sales strategies are implemented in this stage.

- Check the effectiveness of the various strategies. Find out whether they are bringing the desired results or not.

- The sales representatives should be aware of their roles and responsibilities in the organization.

- It is essential for the organization to evaluate the outcome of proposed strategies for any particular department. Organizations depend on KPI also called Key Performance Indicator or simply Performance Indicator to measure the effectiveness of implemented strategies.

- Ask the sales team to submit reports of what all they have done throughout the week. The management must sit with the sales team frequently to assess their performance and chalk out future course of actions.

- Mapping individual performance over time is essential.

3. Sales Process

- Sales representatives should work as a single unit for maximum productivity. A systematic approach results in error free work.

- The management must make sure sales managers follow a proper channel to reach out to the customers. It pays to adopt a step by step approach.

Sales professionals should follow the below mentioned steps for maximum sales and better output. Do not ignore any step.

i. **Initial Contact/Lead**

- Collect necessary data of potential customers once the target market is decided.

ii. **Information Exchange**

- Inform the customers about various product offerings.

- Make the customers aware of your brand and its benefits.

- The information exchange can be either:

Over the telephone or

Face to face interaction with the potential customer.

iii. **Lead Generation**

- Make a list of the people who show inclination towards purchasing your organization's products or services.

- The sales representatives must identify those who have the potential to buy their products.

iv. **Need Identification**

- Fix a meeting with the prospective buyers. Sit with the client and try to find out more about his needs and expectations.

- Suggest them various options which would fulfill their demands.

v. **Qualified Prospect**

- Identify individuals who are keen on purchasing your company's products or services.

vi. **Proposal**

- Once the buyer agrees to purchase particular products, the seller presents a written proposal to him quoting the rates as well as other necessary terms and conditions. Such a document is often called a proposal.

vii. **Negotiation**

- Negotiation is a stage where two parties (buyer and seller) discuss and negotiate for the best deal beneficial to all.

viii. **Closing of Deal**

- This is the stage where the transaction between the seller and buyer takes place. The selling happens in this stage.

ix. **After Sales Service**

- Keep in touch with the customers even after the purchase for higher customer retention.

Sales Management Strategies

The art of meeting the sales targets effectively through meticulous planning and budgeting refers to sales management. Sales Management helps to extract the best out of employees and achieve the sales goals of the organization in the most effective ways.

Let us go through some sales management strategies:

- **Identify goals and objectives of the sales team**. Be clear on your sales targets. Make sure the targets are realistic and achievable. Also assign a fixed timeline to achieve the targets.

- **Know your product well. Understand what benefits end-users would get from your brand**. The marketers must interact with customers to find out more about their expectations from the product as well as the organization. One would not be able to convince the customers unless and until he himself is clear with the benefits of the products.

- **Identify your target market**. Selling techniques and strategies can't be same for all individuals. Each audience has different needs, interests and requirements.

- **Hire the right individual for the sales team**. Remember the sales professionals have a major role in the success and failure of organizations. Recruit individuals who are aggressive, out of the box thinkers and nurture the dream of making it big in the corporate world. Make the sales representatives very clear about their roles and responsibilities in the team. Develop a lucrative incentive plan for them. Incentives and monetary benefits go a long way in motivating the sales team.

- **Don't lie to your customers. It is important to maintain transparency**. Communicate what all your product actually offers. It is unethical to make false promises. Only commit to what you actually can deliver to customers.

- **Know what your competitors are offering**. It is essential to do a SWOT analysis of your organization to know its strengths, weaknesses, threats and opportunities. A marketer must know how his product is better than his competitors.

- **Sales representatives must do their homework before going for a sales call**. One should never go unprepared. Remember the customer can ask you anything and you have to be ready with your answers. The management must promote training sessions at the workplace to upgrade the skills of the sales professionals and expect them to deliver their level best.

- **Devise strategies as per the target audience**. Know your market well. The individuals must be able to relate to your products. The strategies must be formulated in the presence of all. Each one should have a say in the same. Let everyone come out with his suggestions. Be ready with alternate plans if one plan fails.

- **The management must conduct frequent meetings with the sales team to review their performances**. Keep a track on their daily activities. The sales team must prepare Daily Sales Reports (DSR) for the superiors to know what they are up to.

- **One must assess his own performance**. Recall your interactions with the clients and analyze where you went wrong and where things could have been a little better.

- **Treat your customers well for higher customer satisfaction and retention**. Don't oversell. Once you are through with your sales presentation, don't be after your client's life. Give him time to think and decide.

- **The sales pitch must be impressive** for the desired impact.

Sales Operation

Sales Operation refers to various activities which help in the timely achievement of sales targets for the successful functioning of an organization.

Sales Operation includes various strategies and techniques employed by an individual to achieve sales goals within the stipulated time frame.

Why Sales Operation ?

- Sales Operation activities help the sales professionals to meet the sales targets in a systematic and the best possible way.

- Sales Operation activities help to devise relevant strategies and plans (both long term as well as short term) to achieve the sales goals.

- In simpler words sales operation activities help in generating revenues for the organization through meticulous planning, better budgeting and adopting a methodical approach.

Let us go through the various steps in sales operation:

1. **Sales representatives should prepare their own database**. Make sure you have a long list of potential customers. Mere sitting at office doesn't help in sales. Go out in the field, meet people and gather as much information as you can. Put canopies at strategic locations. Networking helps in sales.

2. **The next step is to segregate the data according to age, sex, income** and so on. Classify the data under various sub heads like working/non working, middle class/upper class, employed/unemployed etc. Such classifications help you to understand the customers better and identify your target audience.

3. **Sales strategies ought to be different for every segment.** The needs and interests of a female would be different as compared to a male. Similar products would not excite a youngster and an individual who is 50 years old. Create relevant strategies for different segments as per their needs, interests and demands. The promotional plans must excite the customers and attract them towards the organization.

4. **Speak to the customers and seek for appointment.** Fix up a time as per their convenience. One should never call a customer more than twice in a single day. It irritates him and he tends to avoid you in future. Give him time to think and decide. Avoid being pushy. One can also send a soft reminder through email to the customer.

5. **Once you get an appointment, make sure you reach the venue on time.** Don't expect the customer to wait for you.

Remember the customer can ask you anything related to the product. Make sure you know everything about the product and its offerings.

6. **Understand the needs and expectations of the customers**. Try to make him understand how your product would benefit him? Make him realize how your product is better than the competitor's. Don't oversell.

7. **Attend sales deal with an open mind**. Don't be too rigid on price and other terms and conditions. Give the best deal to the customers for them to come back again to your organization.

8. **Sign a written agreement with the buyer**. The agreement should have the description of the product, model no, date of purchase, warranty details and other necessary terms and conditions. Some organizations also give bills to the customers. Bills are required when the customer comes for an exchange.

9. **Make sure products are delivered in good and working condition to the customers**. It is the duty of the sales representatives to assist the customers in installing, using or maintaining the products.

10. **Make sure you are in touch with the clients** even after the deal for higher customer satisfaction, higher customer retention and eventually higher revenues.

Managing the Sales Cycle

What is a Sales Cycle ?

Sales cycle refers to the various processes which help the products reach the end users. Customers go through a sequence of activities before the product finally reaches them. Such activities are a part of the sales cycle.

A sales cycle has the following steps:

1. Identifying Prospects

- The first step in the sales cycle is to make a list of potential customers.

- Try to gather as much data as you can. Ask your team members to visit markets, shopping malls, restaurants to map potential customers and collect information about them

- Placing canopies at strategic locations also invite potential customers.

- A sales professional should ideally spend his

maximum time outside office meeting people. Interact with as many individuals as you can.

- Distribute questionnaires amongst the potential customers to know them better.

2. Setting Appointments

- The next step is to make the people aware of your product and its offerings.

- Try to get in touch with the people. Call them and seek an appointment.

- Don't arrange meetings at your convenience.

- Take his address and courier relevant information brochures beforehand for him to know more about your product and its benefits.

- Marketers also depend on cold calls to inform the customers about their products and services. Don't be after the individual's life to fix an appointment.

- Do take care of your pitch while speaking over the phone. Make your speech interesting. Don't drag conversations.

3. Know Your Customer Well

- It really helps if you know something about your client before meeting him.

- Try to gain some information about him from social networking sites like facebook, orkut, linked in, twitter and so on. These networking sites do give some information about the client which definitely helps in preparing the sales pitch.

- Understand the customer's needs and expectations from the product. Check whether the customer has the potential to purchase a particular product or not. There is no point selling an air-conditioner to someone whose monthly income is Rs 10000/-. Find out more about the background of the customer.

4. Determine Client's Solution

- Suggest the right option for the customers. A sales representative must never lie to the customers. Say what your product actually offers.

- It is unprofessional to make false commitments. Sit with the customer and help him with the best solutions. Don't always think about your own targets and incentives. Think from the customer's perspective as well. Don't prompt him to buy something which you yourself feel is not right for him.

5. Written Proposal/Document

- Once the customer decides on the product, present a proposal to him with the proposed rates and other necessary terms and conditions.

6. Negotiation Round

- There should always be room for negotiation in deals. Don't be too rigid. Negotiate with an open mind.

- The customers should be aware of even the minutest details. For higher customer satisfaction, give him the best deal.

- A sales professional should always aim to close the deal as soon as both the parties accept the terms and conditions.

7. After Sales Service

- Make sure customers are satisfied with your service.

- Find out whether all his demands are fulfilled or not.

- Be in touch with him even after the deal is over.

What is a Sales Funnel and its Implications for Marketers

Introduction

The sales funnel is a concept that is used to visually describe the sales process from initial leads to final closure. It uses the image of a "funnel" where the opportunities are dropped into the funnel and go through the sieve towards each stage. The opportunities that do not make it to the final stage are described as the "leaky funnel" where they are removed from the funnel and fall by the wayside. On the other hand, the opportunities that are converted pass through the funnel and into the container. The sales funnel is a useful representation of the probability of the leads being converted and hence, it has become quite popular among managers and sales and marketing personnel.

Mechanics of the Sales Funnel

The mechanics of the sales funnel denotes the process of the sale progressing through the funnel in steps and at each step, certain actions have to be taken to actualize the sale. This means that organizations have to handhold each stage of the funnel and this entails targeting clients appropriately and removing the barriers that prevent the opportunity from progressing into the next stage. It is for this reason that organizations develop sales metrics which signify the percentage completion at each stage and which can be used to refine and fine-tune the sales and marketing process through each phase of the funnel. Indeed, the originators of the sales funnel concept recommend organizations to develop their own sales funnels so that instead of relying on the established pattern, which might or might not work for them, they can customize the funnel according to the specific needs of their business.

Stages in the Sales Funnel

The stages in the sales funnel are Lead, Prospect, Qualified Prospect, Committed, and Transacted which when taken together represent the progress of potential sales opportunities through each phase and which might result in actual deals being made. A lead is an opportunity which is the first stage and which denotes approaching clients with whom the organization does not have a relationship and yet, these clients are approached because they fit the profile of the target customer for the organizations.

A prospect is a client who has passed the first stage and has confirmed interest to the organization. However, this stage does not actually translate into actual deals as at this stage, the organization and the client are "talking" which is a sign of progress though the deal is not completed.

The qualified prospect stage is the most demanding and crucial as well as critical stage in the funnel because the organization has moved beyond initial contacts, expression of interest, doing the due diligence and is ready for the talks to progress to the advanced stage. The aspect of due diligence is important as both the organization and the client have established a rapport after ensuring that the client's needs and demands are aligned with the organization's capabilities and the value offered by it. Further, the determination of fit and alignment is also accompanied by the higher ups of each side taking a personal interest in each other as the groundwork has already been completed. Therefore, this stage can make or break a deal and hence, many organizations prepare elaborate presentations and pitches that are not generic but tailored to the client's specific needs.

The committed stage is the move by the organization and client towards closure and this stage is usually the phase when potential red flags that can obstruct the deal have been removed. Moreover, as the name implies, the client has committed to the deal and the organization has prepared for the last mile talks, which are usually held between the division heads or managers depending on the cost of the deal and the potential scope for profits.

The transacted stage represents the closure of the deal and its announcement by both parties. The focus at this stage is on the specifics of how the deal would be actualized through writing of contracts, agreeing upon of delivery schedules, and mentioning the legal options in case of any lapse or slip up on the part of either party. This stage is when contracts are signed and press releases are prepared to announce the deal to the investors and the stock exchanges (if either party or both are publicly listed companies)

The Leaky Funnel

We have seen how opportunities can be converted into actual sales and how the stages of the sales funnel indicate the process of the sales leads and their actualization into real deals. However, not all opportunities are converted into actual deals and if a particular opportunity does not move down the funnel and the sale is not fructified, and then it is known as a leaky funnel opportunity and therefore, must be discarded from the funnel. Of course, this means that the conversion rate takes a hit, which can be a good thing or a bad thing depending on how the organization views that opportunity. For instance, for many organizations, approaching potential clients is a fact of business and this is done through cold calling, which denotes the approach even at the prospect of being rejected. This does not really bother the company since all that their sales and marketing personnel are interested in is to approach clients who can be converted into opportunities at a later point in time. Moreover, once the leaky funnel manifests and the opportunity is removed from the funnel, it gives the organization a chance to focus on potentially profitable leads instead of wasting time in chasing dead ends.

Motivating the Sales Team

Sales Professionals play a pivotal role in generating revenues for the organization. They are the ones who are responsible for product promotion and making a particular brand popular amongst the end users. In simpler words, sales representatives are the true face of an organization.

The individuals representing the sales and marketing vertical must be satisfied with their organization. A sense of belonging at the workplace is important.

Superiors must motivate the sales team from time to time to extract the best out of them.

Let us go through various ways to motivate the sales team:

1. Regular Interaction

- The management must interact with the sales team more often to understand their needs and expectations from the organization.

- The sales representatives must have an easy access to the boss's cabin at the times of queries. Transparency is essential at all levels.

- The sales manager must sit with his team once in a week to address their grievances. No issue should be left unattended.

- Healthy communication between the management and sales team is a good way to motivate the individuals. The sales executives must be aware of the latest developments at the workplace.

- Take them out once in a while for picnics, outings or dinners. Such activities bind the team members together and motivate them to work as a single unit.

2. Roles and responsibilities

- Roles and responsibilities must not be imposed on any of the members. Let them accept responsibilities on their own. It is for the superiors to understand which employee can perform which function in the best possible way. Job mismatch leads to demotivated employees.

- They should be aware of their KRAs from the very beginning. The management should make it very clear that a sales representative is expected to go out and meet clients. No individual should have unrealistic demands. It leads to problems and confusions later on.

- A sales professional must be aggressive, smart and a little diplomatic. They must be excellent in follow ups. Impatient individuals find it difficult to do well in sales.

3. Realistic Targets

- Targets for the sales team must be realistic and achievable. Don't ask for anything which you yourself know is not possible.

- Don't expect miracles overnight.

4. Incentives and Monetary benefits

- Handsome incentive plans go a long way in motivating the sales professionals. Nothing works better than money. Attractive incentive schemes prompt the employees to work hard and make the maximum use of their ability.

- Performers must be rewarded with attractive gifts, coupons, cash prizes or certificates for them to feel motivated and deliver the same performance every time.

- Acknowledge the hard work of employees.

5. Appreciation

- Appreciation plays an important role in motivating the employees. Praise the ones who perform exceptionally well. A pat on their back can actually do wonders. Let them feel special and indispensable for the team as well as the organization. Give them their due credit.

- Display their names on the notice boards for everyone to get a glimpse. Give them badges to flaunt.

6. Involvement

- Involve the team members in the company's strategies. Let them participate in important discussions. Don't criticize their ideas or views.

Roles and Responsibilities of a Sales Manager

A sales manager plays a key role in the success and failure of an organization. He is the one who plays a pivotal role in achieving the sales targets and eventually generates revenue for the organization.

A sales manager must be very clear about his role in the organization. He should know what he is supposed to do at the workplace.

Let us understand the roles and responsibilities of a sales manager:

- A sales manager is responsible for meeting the sales targets of the organization through effective planning and budgeting.

- A sales manager can't work alone. He needs the support of his sales team where each one contributes in his best possible way and works towards the goals and objectives of the organization. He is the one who sets the targets for the sales executives and other sales representatives. A sales manager must ensure the targets are realistic and achievable.

- The duties must not be imposed on anyone, instead should be delegated as per interests and specializations of the individuals. A sales manager must understand who can perform a particular task in the most effective way. It is his role to extract the best out of each employee.

- **A sales manager devises strategies** and techniques necessary for achieving the sales targets. He is the one who decides the future course of action for his team members.

- It is the sales manager's duty to **map potential customers and generate leads for the organization**. He should look forward to generating new opportunities for the organization.

- A sales manager is also responsible for **brand promotion**. He must make the product popular amongst the consumers. A banner at a wrong place is of no use. Canopies must be placed at strategic locations; hoardings should be installed at important places for the best results.

- **Motivating team members** is one of the most important duties of a sales manager. He needs to make his team work as a single unit working towards a common objective. He must ensure team members don't fight amongst themselves and share cordial relationship with each other. Develop lucrative incentive schemes and introduce monetary benefits to encourage them to deliver their level best. Appreciate whenever they do good work.

- It is the sales manager's duty to ensure his **team is delivering desired results**. Supervision is essential. Track their performances. Make sure each one is living up to the expectations of the organization. Ask them to submit a report of what all they have done through out the week or month. The performers must be encouraged while the non performers must be dealt with utmost patience and care.

- He is the one who takes major decisions for his team. He should act as a pillar of support for them and stand by their side at the hours of crisis.

- A sales manager should set an example for his team members. He should be a source of inspiration for his team members.

- A sales manager is responsible for not only selling but also **maintaining and improving relationships with the client**. Client relationship management is also his KRA.

- As a sales manager, one should maintain necessary data and records for future reference.

Qualities of a Sales Professional

Sales Professionals are the face of an organization. They have the responsibility of making the brand popular and promoting the products amongst the end users.

They help in the successful running of organization by generating revenues and earning profits.

Let us go through some qualities which a sales professional must have:

1. Patience

- A sales manager needs to be extremely patient. You just can't afford to be rude to your customers.
- Clients do need time to believe in you and trust your products. Don't get hyper and make the client's life hell. Give him time to think and decide.

2. People Oriented

- It is essential for a sales manager to be customer centric. Understand customer's needs and expectations. Don't simply impose things on him.

- Individuals representing the sales vertical need to be caring and kind towards customers.

- Don't only think about your own targets and selfish interest's. One should never misguide the customers. Be honest with them. Avoid telling lies and creating fake stories.

3. Aggressive

- A sales professional needs to be aggressive and energetic. Lazy individuals don't make great sales professionals.

4. Go-Getter Attitude

- It pays to be optimistic in sales. Sales professionals need to have a go-getter attitude for the best results.

- It is really not necessary that all customers would like or need your product. Don't expect results every time. Remember failures are the stepping stones to success. One must learn from his previous mistakes and move on. Don't take failures to heart.

5. Value Time

- People in sales must value time. Being late for meetings create a wrong impression in the minds of customers.

- It is a sin to make customers waiting unless and until there is an emergency. Start a little early and make sure you reach meetings on time.

6. Sense of Commitment

- A sales representative who is committed towards his work manages to do well and make his mark as compared to others. Commitment in fact is essential in all areas of work.

- If you have promised someone to meet at 5pm, make sure you are there at the desired venue at 4.45 pm sharp. Don't make silly excuses. Trust is lost when commitments are taken back. There should be no turning back.

7. Reliable

- The customers must be able to depend on the sales professionals. A sense of trust is important.

8. Flexible

- A sales professional must know how to change his sales pitch as per the client. Don't just stick to one plan or one idea.

- Learn to take quick decisions as per the situation. Be adaptable to changes. People in sales should not be too rigid and demanding.

9. Be Transparent

- Don't hide things from the customers. Transparency is essential to avoid problems later on.

- Convey only what your product offers.

10. Diligent

- Mere sitting at office does not help in sales. One needs to go out, meet people and make prospective clients. Don't complain if it is too hot or cold outside.

- A sales professional ideally should spend his maximum time in field to achieve targets in the best possible way.

11. Good Communicator

- A sales professional must be a good communicator for the desired impact.

- Take care of your pitch and tone.

Different Types of Sales Professionals

A sales professional in a workplace is responsible for meeting the sales targets of the organization and maintaining relationship with the existing and potential clients.

He plays a central role in generating revenues for the organization.

Following are the types of sales people in organizations:

1. The Diplomat

- As the name suggests, a diplomat is one who always tries to play a safe game. He hates taking risks in life and accepts things as they come.

- These people tend to have a casual approach towards work.

- A diplomat never believes in putting pressure on the customers. If he fails to convince the client in the first attempt, he would never try to do it again. He would simply ignore and try with the next client.

- Such sale professionals are calm, have an easy going attitude and are never under pressure.

2. The Rejection Dreader

- Such sales professionals fear rejections and failures at work. They find it very difficult to accept failures at the workplace.

- They depend more on cribbing and complaining rather than working and getting results.

- Such kinds of people fail to motivate themselves and tend to develop a laidback and negative attitude after a single failure.

3. The Militant Closer

- As the name suggests such sales professionals are extremely aggressive and can go to any extent to get results.

- They are only concerned about their targets and results and hardly think about the needs and expectations of the clients. For them the only thing which matters is closing the deal. They hardly bother whether a customer requires a particular product or not

- In most cases they make the client's life hell just to sell their products and earn revenues.

4. The Sales Scholar

- Such sales professionals believe in lots of research and planning before going for a sales call.

- They spend their maximum time browsing internet, reading books and newspapers, checking various articles on sales rather than going out in the field and meeting people.

- Sales scholars put more emphasis on theoretical knowledge as compared to practical exposure.

- They have an eye on even the minutest details.

5. The Phony

- There are certain sales representatives who simply pretend to be client's best friend. Such people fall in this category.

- They always speak good and appear to be sugar coated.

6. The Overcooked Casualty

- This category involves people who do sales just to earn their bread and butter, not as a passion.

- Such people chose sales as a profession because they feel it is an easy way to earn money as there are huge incentives involved.

- Their main motive is to close deals and earn incentives. They do not care much for the customers.

7. The Professional

- As the name suggests the professionals are the ones who look forward towards providing the right solution to the clients.

- They enjoy interacting with people and suggest only what is right and best for them.

- Professionals ensure clients are satisfied with their service. For them client relationship is of utmost importance.

- They never get impatient or hyper while attending customers instead suggest them the best available options.

Role of Communication in Sales Management

Sales Management refers to the art of achieving the sales targets within the stipulated time frame through effective budgeting and meticulous planning. Sales management enables the sales representatives to close sales deals in favour of the organization and eventually earn revenues for the same.

Communication plays an important role in sales management. Sales professionals need to be good communicators for the desired impact. In simpler words, communication is the backbone of sales management. It is absolutely not possible to close a sales deal without effective communication.

There must be healthy communication between the sales professionals and the customers as well as amongst the sales representatives.

Communication between sales professionals and external clients

Keep your sales pitch simple and precise. Complicated sales terminologies and jargons confuse the customers. It is important for the customers to understand your products for them to believe in them and eventually purchase the same. The sales professionals must be well aware of the benefits of the products.

Sales professionals must be very careful about their tone of voice. Never be too loud or too soft. Be polite. Make sure you are audible to the customers. Don't ever be rude to them.

While addressing a group of customers make sure even the individuals sitting on the last bench can hear you properly. Don't just speak for the front benchers.

One should never interfere when the second party is speaking. Wait for your turn to speak.

Don't play with words. Convey exactly what your product offers. **Fake promises and wrong commitments lead to problems and confusions later on**. Transparency is essential for a long term relationship with the customers. Avoid telling lies to them.

Make sure your sales presentation is interesting.

While speaking to the customers over the phone, make sure you are not chewing or eating something. **Don't put the customers on long holds**. Never avoid customer's calls unless and until there is an emergency.

Understand the needs and expectations of the customers and suggest them the best solution.

The customer can ask you any question under the sun and it is your duty to clarify his doubts. Make sure you are well prepared. One should never lose his temper while interacting with the customers.

Include warm greetings in your conversation for a personal touch.

Communication amongst the sales team

The sales manager must communicate with his sales team on an open platform for everyone to participate and give their valuable inputs and suggestions.

Transparency must be maintained at all levels for healthy relationship amongst the sales professionals. The sales representatives should be aware of their targets and incentives from the very beginning to avoid confusions later on. Make sure the targets are realistic and achievable.

All important information should be circulated through emails. The related members should be kept in loop for everyone to get the same information. Do not communicate with individuals separately in closed cabins. It gives a wrong message Each one should have the liberty to express his/her views and participate in decision making process of the organization

The roles and responsibilities of sales representatives must be communicated to them well in advance. They must know what is expected out of them.

Effective communication is instrumental in closing sales deals and maintaining healthy relationship with the existing as well as potential clients.

Role of Attitude and Personality in Sales Management

The art of achieving the sales targets within the desired time frame through effective planning and budgeting refers to sales management.

Effective sales management ensures timely generation of revenue and profitability of the organization. Sales professionals in simpler words are the face of any organization and have the responsibility of making a particular brand popular amongst the end-users. They are the ones who directly interact with the customers, understand their needs and expectations and try to provide them the best solution.

Attitude and personality play an important role in sales management.

- **Don't go for meetings with a negative mind**. Remember a negative mind leads to wrong thoughts and negativity all around. A cheerful individual spreads happiness all around and leads to a positive ambience at the workplace. It always pays to be optimistic in sales. If one puts his heart and soul in work, the outcome will definitely be in his favour.

- **Don't go for meetings with a negative mind**. Remember a negative mind leads to wrong thoughts and negativity all around. A cheerful individual spreads happiness all around and leads to a positive ambience at the workplace. It always pays to be optimistic in sales. If one puts his heart and soul in work, the outcome will definitely be in his favour.

- **One should always look at the brighter sides of life**. Negativity is all in the minds of individuals. Avoid complaining or cribbing over petty issues. The customer might not think along the same lines as you, but that does not mean you can be rude to him. It is important to be polite and kind to them. Understand what they expect from you and your organization and give them the right suggestion. Make them feel comfortable.

- **One can't achieve results everytime**. It is absolutely okay if one customer does not agree to your presentation and prefers your competitor's offerings. Don't take failures to heart. Remember failure is just the opposite of success.

Never lose hope; instead find out the causes of failure and move on. There is no point crying over spilt milk. Be your own critic, analyze the things and find out what went wrong. Incorporate the necessary changes in your sales pitch for better results next time. Go out, meet people and increase your list of potential customers. Develop a strong network. It helps in sales.

- **Sales professionals should never be shabbily dressed** as they directly interact with the clients. Avoid wearing casuals as customers would never take you seriously. Follow the professional dress code but make sure you don't feel uncomfortable. Don't wear loud clothes to work or for meetings. Ensure you smell good. Foul smell irritates the customer. Do shave before you go for sales deals. Make sure your nails are short and clean. It is essential for sales professionals to look good and clean for the desired impact.

- **Sales representatives ought to be aggressive and have a pleasing personality** Individuals with a laidback attitude should not take sales and marketing as profession.

People in sales should have a charismatic personality to attract and influence the customers.

- **Individuals willing to make a career in sales should be extroverts**. They should love interacting with people. It is important for the sales representatives to break the ice and gel with the customers.

- **Sales representatives should look confident and sound intelligent**. Never show your desperation to the customers. Don't tell them how badly you need to sell the product to meet your targets.

Tips for Successful Sales Professionals

Sales professionals play an essential role in the success or failure of an organization. Their key responsibility areas include promoting a product and making a brand popular amongst the end-users.

Sales representatives earn profits and generate revenues for the organization.

Let us go through some tips for successful sales professional:

- **Understand your product well**. Customers would find it difficult to believe you unless and until you yourself are convinced with the product. Know the benefits of your product or service. Sales professionals must be very clear with the USPs of the products for the customers to believe them.

- **Take pride in your profession**. An individual should not choose sales as a profession just because it is a quick source of earning money in the form of incentives. Individuals should have a passion for sales. Enjoy your work to the fullest for the best results. Never treat your job as a burden.

- **Sales representatives can't afford to be impatient**. Customers would definitely take some time to believe in you and your product but that's absolutely okay. It is a sin to shout or ill treat customers. They must be dealt with utmost patience and care. Be kind to the customers.

- **Interact with the customers more often** and try to find out their needs and expectations. Be honest with people. Suggest them only what is right for them.

- **Create a target market for your products**. Don't try to sell a flat screen television or air conditioner to someone whose monthly income is rupees ten thousand only. It would be a sheer wastage of time, energy and talent. Understand the purchasing power of the customers.

- **Don't oversell**. One should never irritate the customers. Don't make their lives hell. Being pushy never leads to closure of deals; rather it leaves the customers' irritated. Give them time to think and decide. It is good to be aggressive but never cross that fine line.

- **A sales representative must never show his desperation in front of the customers**. Don't show him how badly you need to sell the products to achieve your targets. He has nothing to do with it. If he really needs the product, he would definitely buy it.

- **Be a self motivator**. Set a goal for yourself and try to achieve the same in the best possible way. Give your heart and soul in each deal.

- **Avoid adopting a casual attitude**. Don't go casually dressed for sales meetings. Clients will never take you seriously.

- **Be a good communicator**. Take care of your pitch while speaking to the customers. Avoid being too loud or too soft. Make sure you are audible and the customers understand you.

- **Convey what your product actually offers**. Lies and fake stories cost later.

- **Don't be afraid of the targets**. Accept them only when they are realistic and achievable.

- Sitting in the office doesn't help in sales. Sales representatives must go out and meet people. Make a list of prospective customers. Exchange contact details and visiting cards to reach a wider audience.

- Don't feel bad if you are unable to close a deal. Understand where you went wrong and how things could have been a little better. Be your own critic.

- **Be a good listener**. Listen to what the second party has to say.

Time Management and Planning in Sales Management

Sales management helps in the achievement of sales targets within defined deadlines through effective planning and budgeting.

Through effective sales management, individuals generate revenues and earn profits for the organization.

It is essential for the sales professionals to understand the value of time. One must fulfill commitments and there should be no turn backs in the same.

Time management and Planning play an important role in Sales Management:

- **Managing time well increases productivity** of an individual and also avoids forgetting important things.

- Time management ensures the completion of tasks at a much faster rate and more effectively.

- **Plan your day well in advance**. List out things that are important and need to be done on a priority basis.

- **Prepare a task plan or a TO DO list**. Jot down important things against the time assigned for each activity. Try to finish the work within the stipulated time frame. Tick the activities already done and concentrate on the remaining.

- Develop the habit of using a planner, organizer or desk calendar to avoid forgetting important tasks.

- One of the best ways to manage time is to be organized. The more you are organized, the more quickly you finish off tasks.

- **Avoid keeping stacks of files and heaps of paper at your workstation**. Keep your desk clean and organized. Throw away what you don't need.

- A cluttered desk leads to negativity all around and one tends to waste his maximum time in searching documents and files. Put a label on top of each file. Keep the important documents handy.

- **One must not do any work halfheartedly**. Make sure you put your heart and soul in work to avoid delays.

- Human beings are not machines who can work at a stretch. Everyone needs time to rejuvenate. Do take a break for half an hour anytime during the day. Surf internet, logon to facebook, chat with your friends or do anything you like. Don't think about work during this time. This would help you to concentrate better on work and eventually complete assignments on time. Avoid distractions while working. Don't interfere in your colleague's work or roam around at the workplace.

- **Review your own performance regularly**. Evaluate whether you have finished your work on time or not?

- **Sales professionals should never be late to meetings**. Don't make the customers waiting. It is always better to start a little early to reach the venue on or before time. Make sure you are there at the venue before the customer reaches.

- Prepare an action plan as to how a particular task can be accomplished. Adopt a step by step approach. It is important to first finish one task before starting the next.

- Sales professionals must discuss various options and ideas amongst themselves and devise strategies and techniques to accomplish tasks in the best possible way. Do keep in mind the budgets allocated to each task.

- **Analyze the results and outcomes of previous year's activities and prepare a business plan**. Make sure the business plan is concrete and reflects every individual's future course of action.

- Sales representatives can focus more and concentrate better as a result of effective planning. Planning in most cases makes the future secure.

After Sales Service / Customer Service

Customers are the assets of every business. Sales professionals must try their level best to satisfy customers for them to come back again to their organization.

What is After Sales Service ?

After sales service refers to various processes which make sure customers are satisfied with the products and services of the organization.

The needs and demands of the customers must be fulfilled for them to spread a positive word of mouth. In the current scenario, positive word of mouth plays an important role in promoting brands and products.

After sales service makes sure products and services meet or surpass the expectations of the customers.

After sales service includes various activities to find out whether the customer is happy with the products or not? After sales service is a crucial aspect of sales management and must not be ignored.

Why After Sales Service ?

After sales service plays an important role in **customer satisfaction and customer retention**. It generates loyal customers.

Customers start believing in the brand and get associated with the organization for a longer duration. They speak good about the organization and its products.

A satisfied and happy customer brings more individuals and eventually more revenues for the organization.

After sales service plays a pivotal role in **strengthening the bond between the organization and customers**.

After Sales Service Techniques

- Sales Professionals need to stay in touch with the customers even after the deal. Never ignore their calls.
- Call them once in a while to exchange pleasantries.
- **Give them the necessary support**. Help them install, maintain or operate a particular product. Sales professionals selling laptops must ensure windows are configured in the system and customers are able to use net without any difficulty. Similarly organizations selling mobile sim cards must ensure the number is activated immediately once the customer submits his necessary documents.

- **Any product found broken or in a damaged condition must be exchanged immediately by the sales professional**. Don't harass the customers. Listen to their grievances and make them feel comfortable.

- **Create a section in your organization's website where the customers can register their complaints**. Every organization should have a toll free number where the customers can call and discuss their queries. The customer service officers should take a prompt action on the customer's queries. The problems must be resolved immediately.

- Take **feedback** of the products and services from the customers. Feedback helps the organization to know the customers better and incorporate the necessary changes for better customer satisfaction.

- **Ask the customers to sign Annual Maintenance Contract (AMC) with your organization**. AMC is an agreement signed between the organization and the customer where the organization promises to provide after sales services to the second party for a certain duration at nominal costs.

- The exchange policies must be transparent and in favour of the customer. The customer who comes for an exchange should be given the same treatment as was given to him when he came for the first time. Speak to him properly and suggest him the best alternative.

Customer Relationship Management - Meaning, Need and Steps in CRM

In an organization, sales representatives have the responsibility of creating brand awareness and making products popular among the end users. They are the ones who interact with the customers, understand their requirements and fulfill their needs and expectations.

What is Customer Relationship Management ?

The art of managing the organization's relationship with the customers and prospective clients refer to customer relationship management.

Customer relationship management includes various strategies and techniques to maintain healthy relationship with the organization's existing as well as potential customers. Orgnaizations must ensure customers are satisfied with their products and services for higher customer retention. Remember one satisfied customer brings ten new customers with him where as one dissatisfied customer takes away ten customers along with him.

In simpler words, customer relationship management refers to the study of needs and expectations of the customers and providing them the right solution.

Need for Customer Relationship Management

Customer Relationship Management leads to satisfied customers and eventually higher business everytime.

Customer Relationship Management goes a long way in retaining existing customers.

Customer relationship management ensures customers return back home with a smile.

Customer relationship management improves the relationship between the organization and customers. Such activities strengthen the bond between the sales representatives and customers.

Steps to Customer Relationship Management

- It is essential for the sales representatives to understand the needs, interest as well as budget of the customers. Don't suggest anything which would burn a hole in their pockets.

- **Never tell lies to the customers**. Convey them only what your product offers. Don't cook fake stories or ever try to fool them.

- **It is a sin to make customers waiting**. Sales professionals should reach meetings on or before time. Make sure you are there at the venue before the customer reaches.

- **A sales professional should think from the customer's perspective**. Don't only think about your own targets and incentives. Suggest only what is right for the customer. Don't sell an expensive mobile to a customer who earns rupees five thousand per month. He would never come back to you and your organization would lose one of its esteemed customers.

- **Don't oversell**. Being pushy does not work in sales. It a customer needs something; he would definitely purchase the same. Never irritate the customer or make his life hell. Don't call him more than twice in a single day.

- **An individual needs time to develop trust in you and your product**. Give him time to think and decide.

- **Never be rude to customers**. Handle the customers with patience and care. One should never ever get hyper with the customers.

- **Attend sales meeting with a cool mind**. Greet the customers with a smile and try to solve their queries at the earliest.

- **Keep in touch with the customers even after the deal**. Devise customer loyalty programs for them to return to your organization. Give them bonus points or gifts on every second purchase.

- **The sales manger must provide necessary training to the sales team to teach them how to interact with the customers**. Remember customers are the assets of every business and it is important to keep them happy and satisfied for successful functioning of organization.

Understanding Retail - What is Retail ?

Before understanding the concept of retail, let us first go through few terminologies.

- **Market** - Any system or place where parties are engaged in exchange of either goods or services is called as market. The parties are often called as buyers and sellers. The seller offers his goods or services to the buyer who in return purchases it in exchange of money.

- **Goods** - Tangible (things which can be seen and touched) physical products which are transferred from a seller to the buyer (consumer) to fulfill the latter's need are called as goods.

Jack owned two laptops which he sold to Mike. In this case Jack is the seller while Mike is the buyer. Laptops are the goods which were earlier in Jack's custody and now belong to Mike.

What is Retail ?

Retail involves the sale of goods from a single point (malls, markets, department stores etc) directly to the consumer in small quantities for his end use. In a layman's language, retailing is nothing but transaction of goods between the seller and the end user as a single unit (piece) or in small quantities to satisfy the needs of the individual and for his direct consumption.

Let us understand the concept with the help of an example.

Tim wanted to purchase a mobile handset. He went to the nearby store and purchased one for himself.

In the above case, Tim is the buyer who went to a fixed location (in this case the nearby store). He purchased a mobile handset (Quantity - One) to be used by him. An example of retail.

The store from where Tim purchased the handset must have shown him several options for him to select one according to his budget and need.

From where do you think the store owner (also called the retailer) purchased all the handsets?

Here the manufacturers and the wholesalers come into the picture.

The retailers purchase goods in bulk quantities (huge numbers) to be sold to the end-users either directly from the manufacturers or through a wholesaler.

The Supply chain

Manufacturers.......................Retailers................End   User
(Consumer)

Wholesalers

- **Manufacturers** - Manufacturers are the ones who are involved in production of goods with the help of machines, labour and raw materials.

- **Wholesaler** - The wholesaler is the one who purchases the goods from the manufacturers and sells to the retailers in large numbers but at a lower price. A wholesaler never sells goods directly to the end users.

- **Retailer** - A retailer comes at the end of the supply chain who sells the products in small quantities to the end users as per their requirement and need.

  The end user goes to the retailer to buy the goods (products) in small quantities to satisfy his needs and demands. The complete process is also called as Shopping.

- **Shopping** - The process of purchasing products by the consumer is called as shopping. However there are certain cases where shopping does not always end in buying of products. Sometimes individuals do go for shopping but return home empty handed. Such a shopping is merely for fun and is called window shopping. In window shopping, individuals generally go to the market, check out various options and their prices but do not buy anything. This kind of shopping helps to break the monotony.

Types of Retail Outlets

Retailing refers to a process where the retailer sells the goods directly to the end-user for his own consumption in small quantities.

Types of Retail outlets

- **Department Stores**

  A department store is a set-up which offers wide range of products to the end-users under one roof. In a department store, the consumers can get almost all the products they aspire to shop at one place only. Department stores provide a wide range of options to the consumers and thus fulfill all their shopping needs.

  Merchandise:

  Electronic Appliances

  Apparels

  Jewellery

  Toiletries

  Cosmetics

  Footwear

Sportswear

Toys

Books

CDs, DVDs

Examples - Shoppers Stop, Pantaloon

- **Discount Stores**

Discount stores also offer a huge range of products to the end-users but at a discounted rate. The discount stores generally offer a limited range and the quality in certain cases might be a little inferior as compared to the department stores.

Wal-Mart currently operates more than 1300 discount stores in United States. In India Vishal Mega Mart comes under discount store.

Merchandise:

Almost same as department store but at a cheaper price.

- **Supermarket**

A retail store which generally sells food products and household items, properly placed and arranged in specific departments is called a supermarket. A supermarket is an advanced form of the small grocery stores and caters to the household needs of the consumer. The various food products (meat, vegetables, dairy products, juices etc) are all properly displayed at their respective departments to catch the attention of the customers and for them to pick any merchandise depending on their choice and need.

Merchandise:

Bakery products

Cereals

Meat Products, Fish products

Breads

Medicines

Vegetables

Fruits

Soft drinks

Frozen Food

Canned Juices

- **Warehouse Stores**

A retail format which sells limited stock in bulk at a discounted rate is called as warehouse store. Warehouse stores do not bother much about the interiors of the store and the products are not properly displayed.

- **Mom and Pop Store (also called Kirana Store in India)**

Mom and Pop stores are the small stores run by individuals in the nearby locality to cater to daily needs of the consumers staying in the vicinity. They offer selected items and are not at all organized. The size of the store would not be very big and depends on the land available to the owner. They wouldn't offer high-end products.

Merchandise:

Eggs

Bread

Stationery

Toys

Cigarettes

Cereals

Pulses

Medicines

- **Speciality Stores**

As the name suggests, Speciality store would specialize in a particular product and would not sell anything else apart from the specific range.Speciality stores sell only selective items of one particular brand to the consumers and primarily focus on high customer satisfaction.

Example -You will find only Reebok merchandise at Reebok store and nothing else, thus making it a speciality store. You can never find Adidas shoes at a Reebok outlet.

- **Malls**

Many retail stores operating at one place form a mall. A mall would consist of several retail outlets each selling their own merchandise but at a common platform.

- **E Tailers**

Now a days the customers have the option of shopping while sitting at their homes. They can place their order through internet, pay with the help of debit or credit cards and the products are delivered at their homes only. However, there are chances that the products ordered might not reach in the same condition as they were ordered. This kind of shopping is convenient for those who have a hectic schedule and are reluctant to go to retail outlets. In this kind of shopping; the transportation charges are borne by the consumer itself.

Example - EBAY, Rediff Shopping, Amazon

- **Dollar Stores**

  Dollar stores offer selected products at extremely low rates but here the prices are fixed.

  Example - 99 Store would offer all its merchandise at Rs 99 only. No further bargaining is entertained. However the quality of the product is always in doubt at the discount stores.

Retail Mechanism - How does retail work ?

Retailing is defined as the process of selling merchandise to the consumers for their end use in small quantities. The retailer sells products to the end-users either in single units or in small quantities as per their need and capability.

Retailer................................Consumer

(End   -

User)

Retailing

How does retail work ?

Let us now understand the various ways a consumer can purchase goods from the retailer.

- **Counter service**

As the name suggests, counter service refers to the process of procuring the merchandise from the counter. The buyer does not have an easy access to the merchandise of the store and he can't pick up things on his own. In such a mechanism the buyer has to walk up to the counter and ask for his requirements.

Example

Jewellery Store

Can you go to a jewellery store and pick up things on your own ? No

You need to ask the sales person to show you the sample designs for you to finalize something as per your taste and pocket.

Chemist Shop

Chemist shop does not allow the buyers to simply walk into the store and pick up medicines. One needs to walk up to the counter, show his prescription from the doctor to get the medicines from the retailer.

- **Delivery Service**

The mechanism of shipping goods to the customer's doorsteps is called as delivery service. The end-user does not have to walk up to the store to procure his merchandise; instead the goods are directly delivered to his house through various means of transportation. Delivery service is a boon for the individuals who have an extremely busy life style and do not have enough time to walk up to the store.

Online Shopping

Internet has helped end-users to shop from their homes only. Online shopping sites like Amazon, eBay etc provide a wide range of options to the consumers who can order the desired merchandise through internet. Once the payment is done through debit or credit cards, the goods are delivered at the address the customer requests for. The transportation charges however are borne by the consumer himself.

Order through telephone

Now a days several restaurants and eating joints provide an option of ordering food while sitting at home. The food outlets upload their complete menu in the website providing a wide range of options to the end-users. One can easily place his order over the phone and the food is delivered at his doorstep within no time.

Pizza Hut, Dominos (Promise to deliver hot and crisp pizza within 30 minutes of placing the order)

- **Door To Door Sales:** Door to door sales is a process where the sales person travels from one house to the other and prompts the customers to buy the product. He gives the demo of his product and strives hard to convince the individual to buy the merchandise.

Examples

Eureka Forbes operates on this mechanism where experienced sales professional visits the doorsteps of the potential customers, gives them presentations and influences them to purchase the product.

Telephone companies also sometimes rely on this mechanism to sell their connections.

- **Self Service:** In self service the individuals have the liberty to pick up merchandise on their own and help themselves.

- **Second Hand Retail:** In second hand retail shops the retailer sells second hand goods to the end-users. Such shops generally run for charity where people donate their used merchandise to be resold to the poor and needy free of cost.

Retail Pricing - Different Types of Pricing Models

The sale of goods from fixed points (malls, department stores, supermarkets and so on) to the consumer in small quantities for his own consumption is called as retail. According to the concept of retailing, a retailer doesn't sell products in bulk; instead sells the merchandise in small units to the end-users.

Retail Pricing

Cost Plus Pricing Mechanism

Every organization runs to earn profits and so is the retail industry.

Cost plus pricing works on the following principle:

- Cost Price of the product + Profit (Decided by the retailer) = Final price of the merchandise.

According to cost plus pricing strategy the retailer adds some extra amount to the actual cost price of the product to earn his share of profits. The final price of the merchandise includes the profit as decided by the retailer.

Cost Plus Pricing

- Cost plus pricing strategy takes into account the profit of the retailer.

- Cost plus pricing is an easy way to calculate the price of the merchandise.

- The increase in the retailer price of the merchandise is directly proportional to the increase in the cost price.

- The customers however do not have a say in cost plus pricing.

Manufacturer Suggested Retail Price (Also called List Price or Recommended retail price)

According to manufacturer suggested retail pricing strategy the retailer sets the final price of the merchandise as suggested by the manufacturer.

MSRP

- The retailer sells his merchandise at a price suggested by the manufacturer.

Condition 1

- The retailer sells the product at the same price as suggested by the manufacturer.

Condition 2

- The retailer sells the merchandise at a price less than what was suggested by the manufacturer - Such a condition arises when the retailer offers "Sale" on his merchandise.

Condition 3

- Retailers initially quote an unreasonably high price and then reduce the price on the customer's request to make him realize that a favour has been done to him. A condition of Bargain - where the customer negotiates with the retailer to reduce the price of the merchandise.

Competitive Pricing

The cut throat competition in the current retail scenario has prompted the retailers to guarantee excellent customer service to the buyers for them to prefer them over their competitors.

- The price of the merchandise is more or less similar to the competitor's but the retailers add on certain attractive benefits for the customers. (Longer payment term, gifts etc.)

- The retailers ensure that the customers leave their store with a smile to have an edge over the competitors.

- He tries his level best to offer better services to the customers for a better business in future.

Pricing Below Competition

According to pricing below competition policy

- The price of the merchandise is kept lesser than what is being offered by the competitors.

Prestige Pricing (Pricing above competition)

According to prestige pricing mechanism, the price of the merchandise is set slightly above the competitors.

The retailer can charge higher price than the competitors only under the following circumstances:

Exclusive Brands at the store.

Brand image of the store

Prime location of the retail store

Excellent customer service

Merchandise not available at any other store

Latest Trends

Psychological Pricing

- Certain price of a product at which the consumer willingly purchases it is called psychological price.
- The consumer perceives such prices to be correct.
- A retailer sets a psychological price which he feels would meet the expectations of the buyers and they would easily buy the merchandise.

Multiple Pricing

- According to multiple pricing, the retailer sells multiple products (more than one) for a single price.

- The retailers combine few products to be sold for a single fixed price.

- 3 Shirts for $100/- or 3 Perfumes for $20/- and so on.

Discount Pricing

According to discount pricing, the retailer sells his merchandise at a discounted price during off seasons or to clear out his stock.

Cross Merchandising

Retailing refers to the concept of selling merchandise in small quantities to the consumers for their end use. According to retailing, the individual can walk up to any nearby retail store and purchase products as per his need and pocket in small units for his own consumption.

The display of merchandise at the store plays an important role in attracting the customers into the store. The display of the products at the retail store goes a long way in influencing the buying behaviour of the consumers. The presentation of the products is essential to create that first impression in the minds of the consumers.

Cross Merchandising

Cross merchandising refers to the display of opposite and unrelated products together to earn additional revenues for the store. Products from different categories are kept together at one place for the customers to find a relation among them and pick up all.

According to cross merchandising:

- Unrelated products are displayed together.

- The retailer makes profits by linking products which are not related in any sense and belong to different categories.

- Cross Merchandising helps the customers to know about the various options which would complement their product.

- Cross Merchandising makes shopping a pleasurable experience as it saves customer's precious time.

Examples of Cross Merchandising

- Mobile covers displayed next to mobile phones.

- Recharge coupons with new sim cards

- Batteries with electronic appliances

- Neck ties or cuff links displayed with men' shirt

- Fashion jewellery, rings, anklets, hand bags with female dresses
- Shoe laces, shoe shiners, shoe racks with shoes
- Audio CDs with CD Players

Jenny went to a nearby retail store to purchase a shirt for herself. She picked up a nice blue formal shirt displayed on the mannequin. The retailer was smart enough to add matching trouser, scarf and a handbag to the mannequin (Cross Merchandising). Not only did Jenny purchase the shirt but also the trouser as well as the office bag as she felt the products would complement her shirt.

The customer at the first instance can't really decide what all he needs apart from the products he has already purchased. **Through cross merchandising, the retailer smartly tries his level best to convince the customers to buy additional products apart from his existing list.**

Mike went to a nearby departmental store to purchase cigarettes. He spotted chewing gums displayed along with the cigarettes. He immediately decided to purchase the chewing gums along with his cigarettes which he might need after smoking. Thus cross merchandising (display of cigarettes along with chewing gum) made Mike realize the connection between the products and eventually pick both of them.

Important tips for Cross Merchandising

- The opposite products should be sensibly displayed for the customers to be able to relate them.

- The merchandise should be neatly arranged without giving a cluttered look to the store.

- The merchandise must complement each other to create the desired impact.

- **The retailer must make sure the products have some logical connection with each other**.

  Displaying neck ties with Laptops would make no sense and fail to excite the customers. The customer would purchase either of the two (Either the Laptop or the neck tie) depending on his need but would never purchase both. However if laptop bags are kept with laptops, there are chances that the customer might pick up both the products.

- Use hangers, pegs, mannequins or suitable fixtures to intelligently display the unrelated goods and prompt the customer to pick all of them.

Visual Merchandising

The art of increasing the sale of products by effectively and sensibly displaying them at the retail outlet is called as visual merchandising. Visual merchandising refers to the aesthetic display of the merchandise to attract the potential buyers, prompt them to buy and eventually increase the sales of the store. In simpler words, visual merchandising is the art of displaying the merchandise to influence the consumer's buying behaviour.

The store must offer a positive ambience to the customers for them to enjoy their shopping.

The location of the products in the store has an important role in motivating the consumers to buy them. Sensible display of the merchandise goes a long way in influencing the buying decision of the individual.

The end-user will never notice something which is not well organized: instead stacked or thrown in heaps. Proper Space, lighting, placing of dummies, colour of the walls, type of furniture,music, fragrance of the store all help in increasing the sale of the products.

Lighting is one of the critical aspects of visual merchandising. Lighting increases the visibility of the merchandise kept in the store. The store should be adequately lit and well ventilated. Avoid harsh lighting as it blinds the customers who walk into the store.

The signage displaying the name of the store or other necessary information must be installed properly outside the store at a place easily viewable to the customers even from a distance.

The retailer must be extremely cautious about the colour of the paint he chooses for his store. The paint colour can actually set the mood of the customers. The wall colours must be well coordinated with the carpet, floor tiles or the furnitures kept at the store. Dark colours make the room feel small and congested as compared to light and subtle colours.

The store must always smell good. Foul smell irritates the consumers and he would walk out of the store in no time. Use room fresheners 'or aromatic sticks for a pleasant environment.

The merchandise must be properly placed in display racks or shelves according to size and gender. Put necessary labels (size labels) on the shelves as it help the customers to locate the products easily. Make sure the product do not falls off the shelves as it gives a messy look.

The dummies should be intelligently placed and must highlight the unique collections, latest trends and new arrivals in order to catch the attention of the individual. The dummies should not act as an obstacle and should never be kept at the entrance of the store.

Don't play blaring music at the store. It acts as a hindrance to effective communication and the retailer can never understand what the buyer actually intends to buy.

Select the theme of the store according to the season. Red should be the dominating colour during Christmas or Valentines Day as the colour symbolizes love, fun and frolic. A white theme would look out of place during the season of love. Don't keep unnecessary furniture as it gives a cluttered look to the store.

Why Visual Merchandising?

- Visual Merchandising helps the customers to easily find out what they are looking for.
- It helps the customers to know about the latest trends in fashion.

- The customer without any help can actually decide what he intends to buy.

- It increases the sales of the store and results in increased level of customer satisfaction.

- The customers can quickly decide what all they need and thus **visual merchandising makes shopping a pleasant experience**.

- Visual merchandising gives the store its unique image and makes it distinct from others.

Retail Management - Meaning and its Need

What is management ?

Management refers to the process of bringing people together on a common platform and make them work as a single unit to achieve the goals and objectives of an organization. Management is required in all aspects of life and forms an integral part of all businesses.

Retail management

The various processes which help the customers to procure the desired merchandise from the retail stores for their end use refer to retail management. Retail management includes all the steps required to bring the customers into the store and fulfill their buying needs.

Retail management makes shopping a pleasurable experience and ensures the customers leave the store with a smile. In simpler words, retail management helps customers shop without any difficulty.

Need for Retail Management - Why retail management ?

Peter wanted to gift his wife a nice watch on her birthday. He went to the nearby store to check out few options. The retailer took almost an hour to find the watches. This irritated Peter and he vowed not to visit the store again.-An example of poor management.

You just can't afford to make the customer wait for long. The merchandise needs to be well organized to avoid unnecessary searching. Such situations are common in mom and pop stores (kirana stores). One can never enjoy shopping at such stores.

Retail management saves time and ensures the customers easily locate their desired merchandise and return home satisfied.

An effective management avoids unnecessary chaos at the store.

Effective Management controls shopliftings to a large extent.

- The retailer must keep a record of all the products coming into the store.

- The products must be well arranged on the assigned shelves according to size, colour, gender, patterns etc.

- Plan the store layout well.

- The range of products available at the store must be divided into small groups comprising of similar products. Such groups are called categories. A customer can simply walk up to a particular category and look for products without much assistance.

- A unique SKU code must be assigned to each and every product for easy tracking.

- Necessary labels must be put on the shelves for the customers to locate the merchandise on their own.

- Don't keep the customers waiting.

- Make sure the sales representatives attend the customers well. Assist them in their shopping. Greet them with a smile

- The retailer must ensure enough stock is available at the store.

- Make sure the store is kept clean. Don't stock unnecessary furniture as it gives a cluttered look to the store. The customers must be able to move freely.

- The store manager, department managers, cashier and all other employees should be trained from time to time to extract the best out of them. They should be well aware of their roles and responsibilities and customer oriented. They should be experts in their respective areas.

- The store manager must make daily sales reports to keep a track of the cash flow. Use softwares or maintain registers for the same.

- Remove the unsold merchandise from the shelves. Keep them somewhere else.

- Create an attractive display.

- Plan things well in advance to avoid confusions later on.

- Ask the customers to produce bills in case of exchange. Assign fixed timings for the same. Don't entertain customers after a week.

Category Management

The mechanism of selling merchandise in small quantities from a fixed location directly to the individuals for their end use is called as retailing. The fixed location can be anything like super market, hyper market, department stores and so on.

Merchandise - Merchandise refers to the various products available at the store for sale to the end-users. It is the display of the merchandise which actually attracts the customers into the store.

Let us suppose all the products available at the store are stocked at one place only. Would such a display impress the customers ?

The answer is NO. Presentation of products is essential. As a solution to the above problem, the retailers came out with the concept of category management.

The concept of segregating similar products into separate groups is called as category management. The complete range of merchandise available at the retail store is divided into separate product categories consisting of related products.

Categories in a retail store refer to the various groups which consist of products belonging to a similar family. The retailer smartly displays all the related products together as distinct categories for his as well as the end-user's convenience.

Example

Toothpaste, Tooth Brush, Mouth wash, Tongue cleaner, soap, shampoo, body wash, cosmetics etc, can be displayed together under a single category called personal care section. Vegetables, Fruits, Tinned Food, Juice, meat, dairy products form a single category.

Certain retail stores also classify their merchandise into women, men as well as kids category.

Department stores also have separate categories like: Apparels, Footwear, Jewellery, Electronic appliances, Mobiles, Watches, Home furnishings, house hold appliances and so on.

Category

- The complete range of merchandise at the store is divided into separate groups consisting of related products. Such groups are called as categories.

- Each category is treated as a separate business entity.

- The retailer calculates the profit and loss of each category separately.

- Each category contributes in its own way to the profitability of the store.

- The retailer does not promote a single brand but the complete category.

- The concept of categories has gone a long way in developing a strong bond between the retailer and the supplier.

Why Separate Categories ?

- The classification of products into separate category benefits the customers and makes their shopping a pleasurable experience.

- The customers as per their interest, pocket and need can walk up to the respective categories, check out the various options and decide what to buy and what not to buy.

Eight Step Process of category management

- Define the Category

The retailer must sort out the similar products which can be included in a single category. He must make sure that the products bear a strong connection with each other.

- Role of the Formed Category

- Evaluate the current Performance of the category

- Decide targets for the category.

- Devise an overall Strategy to promote the category.

- Formulate specific steps to increase the sales of the category.

- Implementation of the above steps.

- Review and feedback.

However some retailers find the above process cumbersome and only follow the below five steps:

- Form and Review the category.

- Decide the target consumers of the particular category.

- Planning and formulating strategies for the category.

- Implementation of the above strategies

- Results Evaluation

Category Captains

The retailer generally appoints one individual who supplies all the products of a single category. This individual also called as supplier is known as a category captain.

The suppliers are equally responsible for the category and contribute their level best to maximize the revenue of the particular category. He works in close coordination with the retailer and is responsible for the profit and loss of his assigned category.

Retail Marketing - Tips to Promote a Retail Brand

The mechanism of selling products in small quantities from fixed locations to the customers for their end use is called as retailing.

In the current scenario where the end-user has several options to rely on, it is essential that the retailer promotes his brand well amongst the masses.

Let us go through some **tips to promote a retail brand** well:

Signage

Signboards go a long way in creating brand awareness and promoting a particular brand.

- The signage must display the name as well as logo of the retail store.

- It must be installed at the right place visible to all even from a distance.

- It should not be very small. Small signages fail to attract the customers.

- Choose the right paint colour.

- Don't add unnecessary information. Keep it simple but informative.

- Make sure the signage attracts the customers into the store.

- Choose the right theme.

Advertising

Advertising is a strong medium which influences the buying decision of the customer and prompts him to shop. The retailer must ensure to communicate the USPs of his brand to the target customers well through various modes of advertising. The advertisement must be eye-catching for the end-users to click on them.

Various ways of Advertising

1. Billboards

Billboard is one of the best ways of out of home advertising.

Out of home advertising refers to creating awareness amongst the individuals when they are out of their homes.

- Install hoardings, banners, bill boards at strategic locations such as heavy traffic areas, major crossings, railway stations, bus stands etc to entice the customers. The retailer must ensure that the banners get noticed and bring results.

- Newspapers, Television and radio are also effective ways to promote a brand. Television reaches a wider audience and makes the store popular amongst all.

- The advertisement should be a visual treat, appeal the customers and prompt them to visit the store.

2. Coupons

- Coupons are an effective way of promoting a brand as they offer some kind of financial benefit to the customers in the form of discounts and rebates and thus attracting them into the store.

- Coupons help in furthering the brand image of the retail store without much investment.

- More and more people visit the stores to redeem the coupons, thus making the brand popular.

- Discounts, sale, rebates are good ways to promote a brand.

3. Private Label

- Private label is an effective way to promote one's brand at low costs.

- Products manufactured by one company but sold under another company's brand name are called Private Label Products.

- Create your own website.

- Print your own calendars, diaries, planners, table tops with your store's name, address as well as logo. Such an activity creates awareness among individuals.

- Always keep your visiting cards handy and distribute them to as many people as you can.

- In the current scenario, social networking sites go a long way in promoting brands. Create communities and invite people to join the same.

- Customer loyalty programs help to retain customers and attract new individuals to the store.

- Create a positive ambience at the store. Nothing works better than customer satisfaction in the retail industry. One satisfied customer brings ten new customers along with him.

Role of Advertising in Retail

Promoting a brand is more important than opening a store. It is essential to create brand awareness for the customers to know about the brand's existence. The retailer must strive hard to communicate the USPs (Unique selling Proposition) of the brand to influence the buying behaviour of the customers. In simpler words, advertisements help the end-users to know to which brand a particular product belongs.

Advertisements play a crucial role in promoting a brand and creating its awareness amongst the masses.

They help in creating an image of a particular product or brand in the minds of the potential customers. Such a mechanism is also called Brand Positioning.

What is Advertising ?

Advertising is a medium through which an individual or organization highlights the USPs and benefits of a product or service to influence the buying behaviour of the individuals.

It helps to create a positive image of a particular brand in the minds of the customers and prompts them to buy the same.

Role of Advertising in Retail

- The retailer through various ways of advertising strives hard to promote his brand amongst the masses for them to visit the store more often.

- Advertisements attract the customers into the store. They act as a catalyst in bringing the customers to the stores.

The advertisement must effectively communicate the right message and click on the customers. It should be a visual treat and appeal the end-users.

Advertisements have taglines to create awareness of a product or service in the most effective way.

- The tagline has to be crisp and impressive to create the desired impact.

- The tagline should not be lengthy else the effect gets nullified.

- It has to be catchy.

- It should be simple to memorize.

The moment an individual hears "Just Do it", he knows he has to visit a "Nike Store". That's the importance of a tagline.

Modes of Advertising

1. Nothing works better than promoting a brand through **signboards, billboards, hoardings and banners**

intelligently placed at strategic locations like railway stations, crowded areas, heavy traffic crossings, bus stands, near cinema halls, residential areas and so on. Such advertising is also called as out of home advertising.

Out of home advertising is a way to influence the individuals when they are out of their homes. The hoarding must be installed at a height visible to all even from a distance.

Make sure it catches the attention of the passing individuals and influences them to visit the store.

Keep it simple and make sure it doesn't confuse the customers; instead it should convey the information in its desired form.

2. **Print media** is also one of the most effective ways to promote a brand. Newspapers, magazines, catalogues, journals make the brand popular amongst the individuals. Retailers can buy a small space in any of the leading newspapers or magazines; give their ads for the individuals to read and get influenced.

3. **Television** also helps the brand reach a wider audience. Now a days retailers also use celebrities to endorse their

products for that extra zing. Celebrities are shown using the particular brand and thus making it a hit amongst the masses.

Sachin Tendulkar - the famous Indian cricketer endorses Castrol India, MRF tyres, Adidas, Boost etc.A child gets influenced to drink Boost because his favourite cricketer drinks the same.

4. **Radio Advertisements** also help in creating brand awareness.

5. **Social networking** sites have also emerged as one of the easiest and economical ways to promote a product or brand.

Retail Store Operations

Store Atmosphere

The store must offer a positive ambience to the customers for them to enjoy their shopping and leave with a smile.

- The store should not give a cluttered look.

- The products should be properly arranged on the shelves according to their sizes and patterns. Make sure products do not fall off the shelves.

- There should be no foul smell in the store as it irritates the customers.

- The floor, ceiling, carpet, walls and even the mannequins should not have unwanted spots.

- Never dump unnecessary packing boxes, hangers or clothes in the dressing room. Keep it clean.

- Make sure the customers are well attended.

- Don't allow customers to carry eatables inside the store.

Cash Handling

- One of the most important aspects of retailing is cash handling.

- It is essential for the retailer to track the daily cash flow to calculate the profit and loss of the store.

- Cash Registers, electronic cash management system or an elaborate computerized point of sale (POS) system help the retailer to manage the daily sales and the revenue generated.

Prevent Shoplifting/Safety and Security

- The merchandise should not be displayed at the entry or exit of the store.

- Do not allow customers to carry more than three dresses at one time to the trial room.

- Install CCTVs and cameras to keep a close watch on the customers.

- Each and every merchandise should have a security tag.

- Ask the individuals to submit carry bags at the security.

- Make sure the sales representative handle the products carefully.

- Clothes should not have unwanted stains or dust marks as they lose appeal and fail to impress the customers.

- Install a generator for power backup and to avoid unnecessary black outs.

- Keep expensive products in closed cabinets.

- Instruct the children not to touch fragile products.

- The customers should feel safe inside the store.

Customer Service

- Customers are assets of the retail business and the retailer can't afford to lose even a single customer.

- Greet customers with a smile.

- Assist them in their shopping.

- The sales representatives should help the individuals buy merchandise as per their need and pocket.

- The retailer must not oversell his products to the customers. Let them decide on their own.

- Give the individual an honest and correct feedback. If any particular outfit is not looking good on anyone, tell him the truth and suggest him some better options.

- Never compromise on quality of products. Remember one satisfied customer brings five more individuals to the store. Word of mouth plays an important role in Brand Promotion.

Refunds and Returns

- Formulate a concrete refund policy for your store.

- The store should have fixed timings for exchange of merchandise.

- Never exchange products in lieu of cash.

- Never be rude to the customer, instead help him to find something else.

Visual Merchandising

- The position of dummies should be changed frequently.

- There should be adequate light in the store. Change the burned out lights immediately.

- Don't stock unnecessary furniture at the store.

- Choose light and subtle colours for the walls to set the mood of the walk-ins.

- Make sure the signage displays all the necessary information about the store and is installed at the right place visible to all.

- The customers should be able to move and shop freely in the store.

- The retail store should be well ventilated.

Training Program

- The store manager must conduct frequent training programs for the sales representatives, cashier and other team members to motivate them from time to time.

- It is the store manager's responsibility to update his subordinates with the latest softwares in retail or any other developments in the industry.

- It is the store manager's responsibility to collate necessary reports (sales as well as inventory) and send to the head office on a daily basis.

Inventory and Stock Management

- The retailer must ensure to manage inventory to avoid being "out of stock".

- Every retail chain should have its own warehouse to stock the merchandise.

- Take adequate steps to prevent loss of inventory and stock.

Store Design and Layout - Different Floor Plans and Layouts

Opening a retail store is no joke and requires meticulous planning and detailed knowledge.

Location

Make sure your store is in a prime location and is easily accessible to the end-users. Do not open a store at a secluded place.

Floor Plan

The retailer must plan out each and everything well, the location of the shelves or racks to display the merchandise, the position of the mannequins or the cash counter and so on.

1. Straight Floor Plan

The straight floor plan makes optimum use of the walls, and utilizes the space in the most judicious manner. The straight floor plan creates spaces within the retail store for the customers to move and shop freely. It is one of the commonly implemented store designs.

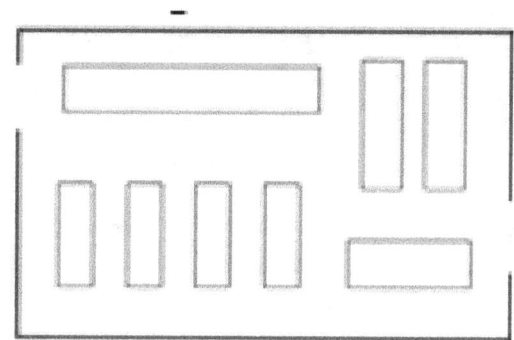

2. Diagonal Floor Plan

According to the diagonal floor plan, the shelves or racks are kept diagonal to each other for the owner or the store manager to have a watch on the customers. Diagonal floor plan works well in stores where customers have the liberty to walk in and pick up merchandise on their own.

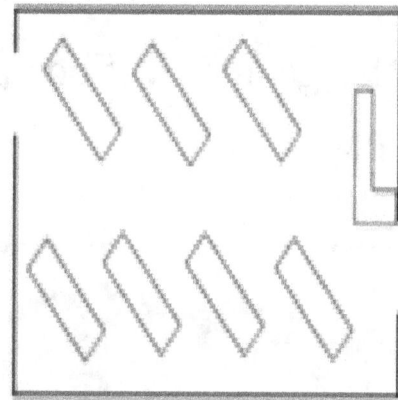

3. Angular Floor Plan

The fixtures and walls are given a curved look to add to the style of the store. Angular floor plan gives a more sophisticated look to the store. Such layouts are often seen in high end stores.

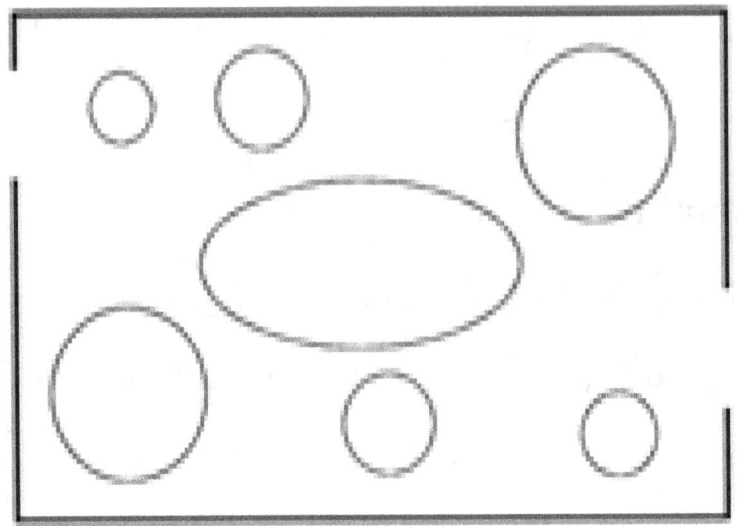

4. Geometric Floor Plan

The racks and fixtures are given a geometric shape in such a floor plan. The geometric floor plan gives a trendy and unique look to the store.

5. Mixed Floor Plan

The mixed floor plan takes into consideration angular, diagonal and straight layout to give rise to the most functional store lay out.

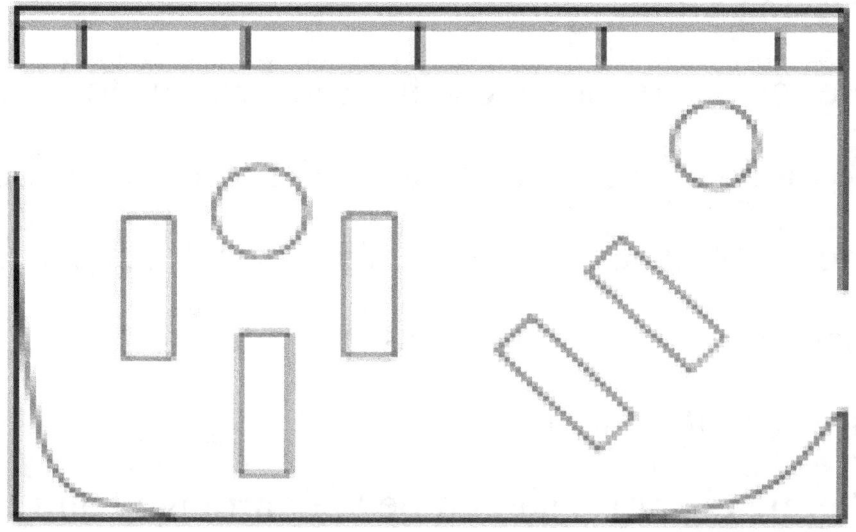

Tips for Store Design and Layout

- The signage displaying the name and logo of the store must be installed at a place where it is visible to all, even from a distance. Don't add too much information.

- The store must offer a positive ambience to the customers. The customers must leave the store with a smile.

- Make sure the mannequins are according to the target market and display the latest trends. The clothes should look fitted on the dummies without using unnecessary pins.

The position of the dummies must be changed from time to time to avoid monotony.

- The trial rooms should have mirrors and must be kept clean. Do not dump unnecessary boxes or hangers in the dressing room.

- The retailer must choose the right colour for the walls to set the mood of the customers. Prefer light and subtle shades.

- The fixtures or furniture should not act as an object of obstacle. Don't unnecessary add too many types of furniture at your store.

- The merchandise should be well arranged and organized on the racks assigned for them. The shelves must carry necessary labels for the customers to easily locate the products they need. Make sure the products do not fall off the shelves.

- Never play loud music at the store.

- The store should be adequately lit so that the products are easily visible to the customers. Replace burned out lights immediately.

- The floor tiles, ceilings, carpet and the racks should be kept clean and stain free.

- There should be no bad odour at the store as it irritates the customers.

- Do not stock anything at the entrance or exit of the store to block the way of the customers. The customers should be able to move freely in the store.

- The retailer must plan his store in a way which minimizes theft or shop lifting.

    i.   Merchandise should never be displayed at the entrance or exit of the store.

    ii. Expensive products like watches, jewellery, precious stones, mobile handsets and so on must be kept in locked cabinets.

    iii. Install cameras, CCTVs to have a closed look on the customers.

    iv. Instruct the store manager or the sales representatives to try and assist all the customers who come for shopping.

    v.   Ask the customers to deposit their carry bags at the entrance itself.

    vi. Do not allow the customers to carry more than three dresses at one time to the trial room.

Signage - Meaning and its Role in Retail Industry

What is a Signage ?

Any visual representation which gives information to the customers about a store, any office, building, street, park and so on is called a signage.

Signage helps the customers to easily reach their desired destination or locate a building by simply following the instructions displayed on it.

Role of Signage in Retail Industry:

- A customer can easily locate the store with the help of a signage.

- **Signboard gives all necessary information about the store**. The customer can easily come to know about the products kept at the store without actually bothering anyone. Visual Displays put inside the retail store can actually help the customers to easily locate the merchandise.

- **It is the signboard which actually attracts the**

customers into the store. The signage should be interesting enough to pull the customers into the store as a retailer can't afford to lose even a single customer.

- The signboard gives the store its unique identity and helps in furthering its brand image.

- A signage goes a long way in influencing the customer's buying decision. A single glance at the signboard helps the customer to decide whether he has to step into the store or not?

Important points to keep in mind while installing Signage

- The signage should never block the entrance of the store. It should not hide the interiors of the store.
- Install the signage at a place which can be easily viewed by all even from a distance.
- The signboard must display all the necessary information like the name of the store, its logo or any other required information.
- Don't put too much information on the signboard. Let the

customers walk into the store and find out on their own what the store is offering.

- A single word "Discount" written on the signboard outside the store can do the trick. The customer would be inquisitive enough to find out what the store offers. He would definitely step into the store to check out the various options. There is actually no need to mention how much discount, what percentage and so on.

- The material and the fabric used for the signboard should be of premium quality so that it lasts for a longer duration. The retailer must make sure the signboard does not lose its lustre.

- Choose the right paint for the signage. Make sure the information is clearly visible to all. The customers should be able to easily read the signboard even from a distance. Choose a light background colour and a dark text colour for clear visibility. One can also highlight the important information. Don't pick any colour which might make your signboard look dull.

- The name of the store should be written in bold or in a

different font to create the desired impact.

- Design your signboard in the most unique and innovative way for the customers to get attracted into the store.

- The signboard should not mislead or confuse the customers.

- Keep the signboard simple but informative.

Role of Coupons in Retail Marketing

What is Retailing ?

The sale of products to the customers from a fixed location (malls, department stores, super markets and so on) in small quantities for their end use is called as retailing. Coupons play an important role in promoting the retail stores and making the brand popular amongst the masses.

What are Coupons ?

Any document which can be presented to the retailer to gain some kind of financial benefit in the form of discount on any product is called a coupon. Customers can get the coupons redeemed at the specific retail outlets to avail relevant discounts and rebates in shopping.

Role of Coupons in Retail Marketing

- Coupons play an important role in attracting the customers into the store.

- Coupons help in furthering the brand image of the retail store without huge investments. It makes the brand popular among the end-users. Individuals talk more about the brand, thus making it a hit amongst the masses.

What is Guerrilla Marketing ?

The concept of promoting products and brands on an extremely low budget is called as Guerrilla Marketing. Guerrilla marketing does not involve huge investments and is one of the most effective ways of creating brand awareness amongst the consumers.

Coupons are an effective tool for Guerrilla Marketing. The retailers can actually create brand awareness amongst the end users without spending much with the help of coupons.

How does Coupons help in Guerrilla Marketing ?

- A Coupon is one of the most cost effective ways of promoting the brand with little investment.

- Coupons make the brand popular as more and more customers visit the store to redeem their coupons.

Example - As a part of their marketing strategy, on every purchase of Domino's pizza, the company offers discount coupons to the buyers. These discount coupons can be availed next time the customer places his order.

In such a situation, it is more likely that he would visit a Domino's Outlet again to redeem his coupons and avail the discounts on the pizza. He would generally not prefer any other outlet as here in Domino's he can get pizza at a lesser price as compared to others.

Dominos in this case used food coupons to attract the customers once again into the store.

- Coupons go a long way in influencing the buying behaviour of the customers.

- Coupons also bring in new customers to the store. The individuals, who do not even know about a particular brand, visit the store to use their coupons and also check out other options as well.

- Coupons also benefit the customers as they can now purchase their desired merchandise at a lower cost.

- Coupons increase the store traffic and also result in Impulse Buying.

What is Impulse Buying ?

Any unplanned buying is called as Impulse Buying. An individual might not require a particular product but picks it up out of mere emotions and feelings. Such a buying is called impulse buying. Impulse buying prompts the customer to purchase products which he might not even need that time.

Peter went to a retail store to redeem his discount coupons on shirts. The retailer had smartly displayed perfumes near the cash counter. While paying the bill, Peter could not resist purchasing two perfumes for himself along with the shirts. An example of Impulse Buying.

Factors Affecting Buying Decision of the Customers at the Store

There are several factors which affect the buying decision of the customers. Let us go through them one by one:

1. **Store Display and Presentation of Products**

The **store display plays an important role in influencing the buying decision of the customers**. It is the display of the store which attracts passing individuals into the store. The store must have an attractive display to entice the customers. Shopping may be the last priority for an individual but a creative display encourages him to spend on shopping.

- A retailer must intelligently display the latest trends on mannequins to prompt the customers to buy the same.

- Make sure the products are kept on their respective racks. The merchandise should not fall off the shelves.

- Since most of us are right handed; we tend to go towards the right side of the store, the moment we step inside. The retailer must thus display expensive and unique merchandise on the right side of the store.
- Remove old stock from the shelves.

2. Ambience of the Store

The **store ambience plays an important role in attracting new customers and retaining existing ones**.

- A customer would never purchase anything from a store which is not clean. Foul smell irritates individuals and thus they leave in no time.
- Play soulful music for a positive effect on the customers.
- The store should be well lit and ventilated for the customers to enjoy their shopping.

3. Customer Treatment

Warm customer treatment is an effective way to pull the

customers into the store. It is essential for the retailers to treat the customers like kings to expect loyalty from them.

- Understand your customers well. Try to find out what they expect from the store.

- The sales representative must greet the customers with a warm smile. It makes a difference.

- Assist them in their shopping.

- Never oversell.

- The retailer must never lie to the customers. If something is not looking good on them, be honest and give them a correct feedback.

- If a customer comes for an exchange, don't be rude; instead help him with an alternative.

4. Store Design and Layout

A customer would never prefer shopping from a store which gives a cluttered look.

- There should be ample space in the store for the customers to move and shop freely.

- Put stickers and labels (size, colour, FS (Full

sleeves), HS (Half Sleeves) and so on) on the shelves and racks.

- Don't stock unnecessary furniture and fixtures in the store.

- Classify the complete range of merchandise into small groups (categories) comprising of similar and related products. Categories help the customers to locate the products easily.

- A store must have a trial (change) room.

- Individuals avoid places where there is a parking hassle. The store should have an adequate parking space.

5. Other Factors

- Discounts and rebates influence the customers to shop more. A customer might not need a product, but a discount will encourage him to purchase the same as he would now get it at a lower price.

- Promotional schemes like free gifts also affect the buying decision of the customers. A Free T Shirt with a pair of jeans would definitely prompt the customers to shop more.

- Customers also indulge in shopping to redeem their coupons and avail discounts.

Tips to be a Successful Retailer

- Opening a retail store is no joke. It demands dedication, detailed study and meticulous planning. An individual must do his groundwork well. **Plan things well in advance to avoid problems later on**.

- It is important to do some kind of research work before taking the big leap. **Browse through related websites to gain an in-depth knowledge**.

- **An individual must be well aware of the fundamentals of retail industry to have an edge over others**. Short term courses in retail make an individual well versed with the basic concepts of retailing, store formats, visual merchandising and so on which eventually help him in the long run.

- **Know what is happening around you**. Keep yourself updated with the latest trends in the retail industry. Check out various fashion magazines, brochures, catalogues, newspapers for the latest developments.

- **Know your target market well**. Find out more about the tastes and preferences to meet their expectations.

- It is important to **choose the right location for the store** to ensure maximum walk-ins. Make sure the store is well connected by means of transportation. Don't open store at a secluded place.

- Make sure there is **adequate parking space** near your store.

- **Promote your store well**. It is essential to create awareness of your brand amongst the customers for them to know about the brand's existence. Devise strategies to make your brand popular amongst the masses.

- Create the company's website and get your visiting cards printed.

- **Set a budget for everything**.

- The products stocked in the store and their display play an important role in attracting the customers into the store. **A retailer must never compromise on quality of the merchandise**. Visit various wholesalers to check out the latest trends. Pick up something which is unique and not available at any other store. Don't stock things which are out of fashion. The merchandise should be as per the target market and location of the store.

• Visit few other retail outlets to get an idea about store designs and layouts.

• Hire trained employees for your store. The employees must be well aware of their roles and responsibilities for them to deliver their best. Motivate them from time to time through various training programmes, appraisals, incentives and other monetary benefits.

• Be patient and don't rush into things.

• **Plan your store layout well**. Make sure there is ample space inside the store for the customers to move and shop freely.

• Don't dump products. Use shelves, cabinets and almirahs to stock your merchandise.

• **Be disciplined**. Open your store on time and assign fixed timings for lunch and tea.

• **Treat your customers as kings**. Advise all the store members to be courteous with the customers. The sales representatives must assist the customers in their shopping and make sure they leave the store with a smile.

- **Never oversell**. Let the customers decide on their own what would look good on them.

- **Manage your inventory well**.

- It is important for the retailer to track the cash flow.

Inventory Management in Retail Industry - Need and Important Terminologies

What is Inventory Management ?

Inventory refers to the goods stocked for future use. Every retail chain has its own warehouse to stock the merchandise to be used when the existing stock replenishes.

Inventory management refers to the storage of products to be used at the time of crisis.

The retailer keeps a track of the stocked goods and makes sure there is surplus inventory to avoid being "out of stock". Such a process is called as inventory management.

Why Inventory Management ?

Gone are the days when customers had limited options for shopping. In the current scenario, if a customer does not find the desired merchandise at one retail shop, he has a second brand to rely on. A retailer can't afford to loose even a single customer. It is really important for the retailer to retain his existing customers as well as attract potential buyers. The retailer must ensure that every customer leaves his store with a smile. Unavailability of merchandise, empty shelves leave a negative impression on the customers and they are reluctant to visit the store in near future. Inventory management prevents such a situation.

One must understand that the products need some time to reach the store from the supplier's unit. The retailer must have sufficient stock to offer to the customers during the "lead time".

Managing inventory also helps the retailer during situations beyond control like transport strikes, curfews etc. The retailer has ample stock as a result of judicious inventory management even at the time of crisis.

Important Terminologies used in Inventory management

1. SKU (Stock Keeping Unit)

Every product available at the store has a unique code. This code which helps in the identification and tracking of the products at the retail store is called as stock keeping unit or SKU.

The retailer feeds each and every SKU in the master computer and can easily track the product in the stock just by entering the SKU Number.

Assigning a unique code to the products avoids unnecessary searching.

Example

Let us take the example of "Numero Uno" which stocks denims, shirts, T Shirts and targets both men as well as women.

SKU for Shirts

- NU – M–40-FL-W

- NU - M-38-FL-B

Where:

NU	stands	for	Numero	Uno
M		-		Men
40	-		Collar	Size
FL	-		Full	Sleeves

W - White (Colour of the shirt)

In the same way B in the second example would stand for Blue

Simply typing NU – M–40-FL-W would let the retailer know whether the particular merchandise is available with him or not.

2. **New Old Stock (Abbreviated as NOS)**

The stock which is never been sold by the retailer and now not even being manufactured comprises the new old stock. Such products do not have takers and may not be produced anymore.

3. Stock out

Stock out refers to a situation when the retailer fails to fulfill the customer's requirement due to lack of merchandise. The merchandise is not available in the current inventory and thus the customer has to return home empty handed.

Preventing loss of inventory

Employees working at the store might get tempted to steal the merchandise.

Let us go through some tips which help to prevent loss of inventory:

- Check the bags of the employees before they leave the store.
- Raise an alarm whenever you find someone stealing something. Supporting a wrong deed is also a crime.
- Make sure that all the employees leave from one common door.
- Avoid multiple exits.

- Check garbage before dumping.

- Keep proper record of the inventory(Stock coming in and going out)